Also by Joe Lamport

Dinkelmann's Rules: a dot comedy of errors
The Life and Times of Richard Musto
The Adventures of Monkey King (translation)
April Poems
A Sutra for Weesuck Creek

All author proceeds from sales of this book will be donated to the Karuna Fund established by the Upaya Institute and Zen Center in Santa Fe, NM. Upaya is a Zen Buddhist practice and educational center dedicated to the development of the relationship between traditional Buddhism and compassionate engagement with the contemporary world. The Karuna Fund honors the practice of Roshi Joan Halifax, the founder of Upaya.

You can learn more about Upaya at the center's website:
http://upaya.org

The Poetry of Awakening

An Anthology of Spiritual Chinese Poetry

Translated by Joe Lamport

Fomite
Burlington, VT

Copyright © 2021 Joseph Lamport
The Sixth Patriarch Cutting the Bamboo (六祖截竹圖), Liang Kai (梁楷, c.1140-1210), Song Dynasty (960-1279)

ISBN-13: 978-1-953236-22-7
Library of Congress Control Number: 2021942540

All rights reserved. No part of this book may be reproduced in any form or by any means without the prior written consent of the publisher, except in the case of brief quotations used in reviews and certain other noncommercial uses permitted by copyright law.
Fomite
58 Peru Street
Burlington, VT 05401
www.fomitepress.com
9/14/2021

For Du Fu —

Only by reading you in Chinese did I discover the path to poetry
through direct struggle, gleaning feeling first,
before puzzling out each character's meaning

I am the madman of Chu
Who sang for Confucius
And laughed at him too
All the while
In both my hands
A precious jade staff
Tightly I clasped

From The Song of Lu Mountain by Li Bai

Contents

Translator's Preface

The Spiritual Heritage   1

Early Buddhist and Daoist Poetry   17
   Xie Ling Yun   21
   Master Fu Daishi   25
   Chen Z'iang   27
   The Chan Origin Story in Verse   41

Poems of the Literati   47
   Yuan Jie   53
   Li Bai   57
   Wang Wei   65
   Bai Juyi   75

Poems by Hermits, Monks and Chan Masters   83
   Shide   91
   Feng Gan   97
   Master Yongjia Xuanjue   101
   Chan Master Hsiang-yen   105
   Jiaoran   107
   Layman Pang   133
   Jia Dao   135
   Qi Ji   141

Glossary   149

Translator's Preface

The 78 poems I have chosen to translate and bring together in this collection were written in China during the first millennium of the Common Era. They include poems by a diverse group of writers, many of them Buddhists of one stripe or another, others Daoists or fellow travelers of the Buddhist faith. But even among those who identified as practicing Buddhists, it may be misleading to suppose much commonality of faith: Buddhist spiritual beliefs and practices in China evolved considerably over the course of the centuries in which these poems were written. Some of the poets collected here were renowned and avowedly secular, while others lived as reclusive hermits, and still others took up orders and lived as members of a monastic community.

Diverse as this grouping of poets may be, and divergent as their life experiences and doctrinal beliefs were, the poems here represent a singular and quite remarkable *poetic* tradition, which I refer to as the poetry of awakening. The common aspiration was to express through poetry the nature of spiritual awakening, as they experienced it in their own lives. These are personal poems, deeply felt, which makes them accessible, even though they speak to us from a distant time and strange culture, and address the loftiest and most abstruse of themes.

At bottom, this tradition rests on an unresolvable paradox. The assumption (often explicitly stated) of these poets is that the experience of spiritual awakening is incapable of being expressed in words, no matter how artfully a poem may be crafted. The insights possessed by the awakened mind and heart simply fall beyond the capacity of language. Why write such poetry at all, then? The wonder of this tradition is the continued striving to give voice to the inexpressible. The tension wrapped up in this paradox confers to the poems' spiritual depth and power.

Something else I find distinctive about this mode of living and writing is the fusion of poetry and spirituality into part of an integrated practice. At their best, these poems are not simply exercises of poetic imagination, nor are they merely descriptive of the poet's spiritual life. They seem directly integrated into the process of spiritual exploration and experience. Poetry becomes the practice. These are not doctrinal poems even though they occasionally include explicit references to elements of Buddhist doctrine, such as the Three Realms* and the Five Aggregates*. It should not diminish your enjoyment of these poems if you know nothing about such matters. It is far more useful to think of them as a form of meditation, as if they were composed through a process closely aligned with meditation — as if the poet were meditating out loud, or with brush and ink close to hand.

*****

This fusion of poetry and spiritual practice is quite distinctive, and not something that emerged to a similar extent in other cultures. Rumi, Meera Bai, and many others around the world have written great mystic verse, but what seems unique in the Chinese tradition is the way that poetry was not simply the preferred mode of expression for a handful of talented and spiritually inclined poets, but rather became accepted and valued in the spiritual tradition itself. Over the course of centuries, poetry in China became a preferred means for adepts to describe the experience of spiritual awakening and other aspects of their day-to-day practice. Instead of being viewed as a means of achieving recognition for possessing literary talent, poetry served as an important means of sharing and expressing a practitioner's faith.

Such fusion of poetry and spiritual practice flourished because of the unique cultural circumstances that arose and prevailed in China during the first millennium, the confluence of two very remarkable cultural developments: the flowering of Tang poetry and the emergence of Chan Buddhism.

Tang Poetry: Poetry had long played a central role in Chinese culture, going back to the Book of Odes, which stood as one of the pillars of early Chinese civilization. But with the ascendance of the first Tang emperor in the early 7th century, China's poetic tradition began to undergo a phenomenal transformation, and poetry to assume an even more commanding cultural significance. The recitation and composition of poetry became an essential part of literacy and stood as one of the major requirements for entry and advancement in government service. As a result, a class of literati with a passionate interest in poetry emerged, many of whom served throughout the Imperial bureaucracy. In the following 200 years, Chinese poetry flourished as never before, as new poetic forms emerged, and poets began to express a far greater range of themes addressing social and political topics, as well as spiritual and deeply personal matters. This was a period of bountiful creativity, perhaps the greatest golden age in history for the art of poetry. The most definitive collection of Tang poems (compiled in China during the early 18th century) contains more than 50,000 poems from more than 2,200 authors. Emperors and ministers, minstrels and monks all wrote poetry. There were women poets, drunken poets and child poets, poetry practiced in schools and among circles of friends. Poetry permeated the entire culture and became an integral part of every educated person's life. And not surprisingly, the poets of this period include some of the greatest of all time, including Wang Wei and Bai Juyi, some of whose poems are included in this collection. A hallmark of Tang poetry is that personal experience becomes a major focus of poetic expression.

Chan Buddhism: Buddhist teachings first began to find their way over the Himalayas into China as early as the third century BC. As the volume of traffic between China and India increased in the next few hundred years, so too did the flow of Buddhist wisdom, as Sanskrit scriptures and sutras were translated into Chinese in the first and second centuries, CE. By the 4th and 5th centuries, Buddhist learning had begun to circulate widely enough among China's educated elite to support the emergence of the first Chinese variants of Buddhism — the Pure Land, TianTai, and the Huayan schools — each of which was heavily influenced by different aspects of the Indian teachings. Then in the late 6th and early 7th century, coinciding with the rise of the Tang Dynasty*, Buddhism in China underwent a complete transformation with the emergence of Chan Buddhism. Chan represented a sharp departure from earlier Chinese variants of Buddhism inasmuch as it rested upon an utterly unique synthesis of Buddhism and Daoism, China's indigenous spiritual tradition, and thus presented itself — and flourished — as something far more homegrown.

A full description of Chan is beyond the scope of this preface or of any other single book. As the Chan tradition evolved, and was subsequently transmitted from China to Japan, it was eventually introduced to a western audience in the mid 20th century through the good offices of T.D. Suzuki and Alan Watts. Contemporary readers may be familiar with it under the name of Zen. Going back to its medieval origins in China, this incredibly rich mixture of Daoism and Buddhism gave birth to an approach to spirituality the likes of which the world had never before seen, a way of thinking about spirituality that prioritized personal experience over received tradition. As the Chan masters proclaimed, *If you see Buddha on the road, kill him*. In place of studying sutras and scripture, Chan disciples pursued spiritual awakening through silent meditation — or just sitting.

The poetry of awakening, then, emerges directly from these two cultural phenomena. On the one hand, Tang Poetry greatly expanded the possible range of poetic expression; on the other, Chan Buddhism directed practitioners' attention away from sutras and scriptures to the realm of personal experience in meditation. The poems collected in this anthology are part of the outpouring resulting from the confluence of these streams of thought and experience.

There are two distinct types of poets whose work is included in this collection. First, there are those known primarily as literati, who spent most of their lives in the secular realm, usually supporting themselves through service in the Imperial bureaucracy. Typically, they were poets first and foremost, who showed a growing interest in spiritual matters towards the end of careers, when they retired or fell out of favor in court. Alternatively, there are those who early on dedicated themselves to spiritual pursuits, choosing to live as hermits or monks, spiritual seekers whose spiritual practice subsequently drew them to writing poetry. Different as the life of a poet-bureaucrat and a poet-monk may have been, they met somewhere in the middle to establish this unique genre, where self-expression through poetry ends up directly entwined with the pursuit or experience of spiritual awakening.

It's important to note that combining Tang poetry with Chan spiritual practice subtly changed the nature of both. As Tang poets became spiritualized, they began to diverge from the literary norms of the period inasmuch as they adopted a far more skeptical view about the adequacy of language to convey their experience. At the same time, as Chan practice became aestheticized, it diverged from customary forms of meditation practice, breaking the silence, as it were, as monks and hermits devoted themselves to composing literary verse. In this way, the poetry of awakening brings us to a unique terrain, which falls somewhere in the area of overlap between the two traditions from which it emerged. The poetry of awakening, whether composed by poet-bureaucrats or poet-monks, represents a hybridization of spiritual and literary elements, to create a distinct form of practice in itself. Crazy words and flowery utterances (狂言绮语) is the way Bai Juyi summed up the genre (of which he was one of the foremost practitioners), reflecting the transgressive nature of these poems.

* * * * *

The joys of reading and translating classical Chinese poetry lie in the sense of unending discovery. Over the millennia there have been countless poets who recorded their spiritual journeys in poem and song. Their surviving written work gives us insight into dharma* paths of incomparable variety and richness, the very opposite of dry religious doctrine or dogma. Each of the poems and poets in this collection brings the dharma alive with distinctive flair, personality and vision. In that sense, ancient as these poems may be, they remain vital sources of inspiration for us in our day-to-day lives as we forge our own spiritual paths, evidence that spiritual awakening may be both ineffable yet within the realm of human speech.

The placement of an asterisk next to a word in the text indicates that there is a brief explanatory entry included in the glossary in the back of the book. I've tried to keep the glossary and headnotes to a minimum in the hopes that the poets and their poems may that better have a chance to speak for themselves.

Joe Lamport
East Quogue, NY

The Spiritual Heritage

The Dao De Jing is one of two foundational texts in Daoism. Lao Tzu is credited as the author. He is thought to have been more or less a contemporary of the Buddha. While not written in the form of poems, the text of the Dao De Jing is remarkably concise and otherwise evinces a strong poetic sensibility in its heavy reliance on metaphor as a means of conveying meaning.

一章

道可道
非常道
名可名
非常名

無名天地始
有名萬物母
常無欲觀其妙
常有欲觀其徼
此兩者同出而異名
同謂之玄玄之又玄
眾妙之門

I

The Dao as spoken
Is ever changing
Names once named
Don't stay the same

Heaven and Earth
Both nameless at birth
Once named gave birth
To ten thousand things*

Ever without desire
Behold the intricate beauty
Ever desirous
Remain strictly bounded

Both ways of being
End the same way
Although differently named
Identity speaks of mystery
Mystery begets more mystery
As it emerges through
The gateway of being

五章

天地不仁
以萬物為芻狗
聖人不仁
以百姓為芻狗

天地之間
其猶橐籥
虛而不屈
動而俞出
多言數窮
不如守中

5

Heaven and Earth
Are without compassion
Looking down on all
Ten thousand things*
As straw dogs easily hewn
The Holy Sage likewise
Lacks compassion
Seeing human ties
The same way too

Heaven and Earth
Are aligned like
A bellows or flute
Hollow but straight
Down the middle
A breath applied soon
Emerges at the other end

But it's not the same
With words
Greater in number
More paltry they seem
Because meaning
Gets lost in the middle

十一章

三十輻共一轂
當其無有
車之用
埏埴以為器
當其無有
器之用
鑿戶牖以為室
當其無有
室之用
有之以為利
無之以為用

11

Thirty spokes
Joined together in a hub
Out of the Nothing
The cart finds use
Clay and water
Shaped into a vessel
Out of the Nothing
The vessel finds use
Chisel to lintel
The room takes shape
Out of the Nothing
The room finds use
In the Something that's good
From the Nothing comes its use

There are dozens of Buddhist sutras that have played an important role in shaping Mahayana Buddhism* generally and the Chan tradition more specifically. But none has been more central to the Chinese Buddhist canon than the Heart Sutra, which is part of a much vaster collection of sutras known as the Prajñāpāramitā or Perfection of Wisdom Sutras. What appears below is a translation of a version of the Heart Sutra, which, according to recent scholarship, was composed by the Tang monk Xuanzang, and which has been described as presenting a condensed version of the much vaster work.

觀自在菩薩
行深般若波羅蜜多時

照見五蘊皆空

度一切苦厄 舍利子

色不異空
空不異色

色即是空
空即是色

受想行識
亦復如是 舍利子

是諸法空相
不生不滅
不垢不淨
不增不減

是故空中
無色
無受想行識
無眼耳鼻舌身意
無色聲香味觸法
無眼界乃至無意識界
無無明 亦無無明盡 乃至
無老死 亦無老死盡
無苦集滅道
無智亦無得 以

The Heart Sutra

The Bodhisattva* Guan Yin
While meditating upon
The Perfection of Wisdom Sutra

Saw clearly
How the Five Bundles
Each and every one of them
Is completely Empty

Everything passes
All suffering
And distress
It's nothing but
Ashes and dust

Form is
No different
Than Emptiness

Emptiness is
No different
Than Form

Form is identical to Emptiness
Emptiness is identical to Form

Feeling
Perception
Willfulness and
Thinking
Are all the same too
Nothing more than
Ashes and dust

無所得故

菩提薩埵 依
般若波羅蜜多故 心
無罣礙
無罣礙故
無有恐怖
遠離顛倒
夢想
究竟涅盤

三世諸佛
依般若波羅蜜多
故 得阿
耨多羅
三藐三菩提
故知般若波羅蜜多
是大神咒
是大明咒
是無上咒
是無等等咒
能除一切苦
真實不虛
故說般若波羅蜜多咒
即說咒曰

揭諦
揭諦

波羅揭諦
波羅僧揭諦
菩提薩婆訶

All the teachings
Of Buddha are Empty too
Unborn and undying
Unblemished and impure
Neither increasing
Nor diminishing

In the midst of Emptiness
There is no Form
Nor is there feeling
Sense perception
Volition nor
Thinking

Without eye ear nose
Tongue finger or mind

Without shape sound smell
Taste texture or learning

Without the visible realm
Without even unconscious thought

Without delusion and also
Subject to delusion without end

And even without age and death
But also subject to age and death
Without end

Without the Four Noble Truths*

Without wisdom and also
Without means to attain wisdom
As no such thing is attainable

The Bodhisattvas all relied
On the Perfection of Wisdom Sutra
Fixed in the their hearts
Without hindrance
Without obstruction
Without fear
Far from confusion
And illusion
In the end
To attain Nirvana

Indeed the Buddhas
Of all Three Realms*
Depended on the
Perfection of Wisdom
Sutra to attain
Supreme Enlightenment
For all Eternity

The Perfection of Wisdom Sutra
It is the holiest mantra
The clearest mantra
There is none higher
A mantra unequalled
The mantra to end all suffering
Truly without a false syllable
In the entire chant

The Perfection of Wisdom Sutra
Chant it thus

Gate
Gate
Paragate
Parasamgate
Bodhi svaha

Early Buddhist and Daoist Poetry

Hui Yuan

The tradition of spiritual poetry in China has a long history that can be traced back even prior to the advent of Chan Buddhism in the Sixth century. One of the very first Buddhist poets was a monk named Hui Yuan whose dates are given as 334-416 AD, which means he pre-dated Bodhidharma's arrival in China by more than two centuries. Hui Yuan is designated as the first patriarch of the Pure Land school of Buddhism and is credited as the builder one of the earliest monastic communities on Mt. Lu, which is considered a sacred spot by Pure Land practitioners down to the present day.

游廬山
慧遠

崇岩吐清氣
幽岫棲神跡
希聲奏群籟
響出山溜滴
有客獨冥游
徑然忘所適
揮手撫雲門
靈關安足闢
流新叩玄扃
感至理弗隔
孰是騰九霄
不奮沖天翮
妙同趣自均
一悟超三益

Wandering on Mt. Lu

On a cliff sublime
That emits the purest *qi*
In a cave remote
Dwelling amidst
Traces of divinity
I hear the music of
A flute that resounds from
The surrounding peaks
And fades away beneath
A solitary guest wandering
From the lower depths
Has found the right path
To pursue forgetfulness

Here I raise my hands and
Caress the cloudy gate
Alert yet cloaked in peace
Surpassingly open
As what flows forth is
A knock unheard before
Upon the mysterious gate
A sense of arrival at what
Is inseparable from
The essence within
Which soars to
The ninth heaven
Without the slightest effort
Buoyant as a feather
How exquisite to be
So much at one
To attain all three realms*
In a single transcendent leap

Xie Ling Yun

Xie Ling Yun was one of the best-known poets in the Six Dynasties period and thus also predated the development of Chan Buddhism. Known for his nature-inspired poems, he was also a lifelong practicing Buddhist and is thought to have been spiritual follower of Hui Yuan. The following verses are excerpted from a longer work Xie wrote as an inscription for a painting of the Buddha's Shadow, which had been commissioned by Hui Yuan and was hung in a cave on Mt. Lu.

群生因染
六趣牵缠
七识迭用
九居屡迁
剧哉五阴
倦矣四缘
遍使轮转
苦根迍邅
迍邅未已
轮转在己
四缘云薄
五阴火起

疊疊正觉
是极是理
动不伤寂
行不乖止
晓尔长梦
贞尔沉诐
以我神明
成尔灵智
我无自我
实承其义
尔无自尔
必袪其伪

Inscription for the Buddha's Shadow

The entire human flock bears
The stain of causality
Entangled in the six paths
Through seven levels of knowing
One from another flowing
And ever changing nine abodes
The five aggregates* and
Their constant interplay
The four sorts of karma
Exhausting us in the extreme
So the wheel of existence
Keeps on turning
Suffering never
Loosens its grip
We keep on stumbling
We too keep turning
Clouded by karma
Our senses inflamed

Relentlessly advancing
Striving for awakening
To reach the extreme
Or to attain the essence
To move while remaining
Silent and inured
Or to go forward
In disarray
Dawn arrives and
Our dream persists
Chaste though submerged
In delusion's depth
Yet I am by the divine
Possessed

Become thus alive
And knowing
I am without self
Truly by spirit blessed
You may be selfless too and
Thus liberated from delusion

Master Fu Daishi

Fu Daishi was a Buddhist monk of the 6th century. He is best known for a wordless lecture on the Diamond Sutra he delivered to the Chinese Emperor Bu-tei. Here is a short poem also attributed to him that anticipates the cryptic and compressed style of koans that later became a staple of the Chan tradition.

空手把鉏頭
步行騎水牛
人在橋上過
橋流水不流

The Bridge that Flows

Empty handed
Grab the handle
Of the hoe

Walk forward
Riding atop
A water buffalo

A man stands
On the bridge
Crossing over

It's the bridge
Not the water
That is flowing

Chen Z'iang

Along with the development of Buddhist-themed poetry, Daoist-themed poetry begins to emerge in the 7th century, as one of several new styles developing in the early years of the Tang Dynasty. Most notably, the poet Chen Z'iang composed a cycle of 38 poems called the Gan Yu, which is steeped in Daoist imagery and symbolism. The overall theme of the Gan Yu cycle is the poet's pursuit of awakening against the backdrop of his travels in the world. One of the distinctive features of the Gan Yu is the poet undertaking a journey, in both a real and metaphorical sense, as part of the spiritual quest.

感遇 其一

微月生西海
幽阳始化升
圆光正东满
阴魄已朝凝
太极生天地
三元更废兴
至精谅斯在
三五谁能征

Gan Yu - 1

The moon declines
Into the western sea
To be reborn anew

The sun's journey
Has almost begun
Soon to be ascendant

Bright radiance
Fills the East
The sky bursting

Yet cloudy is the soul
At the moment of dawn

So the Ultimate gives birth
To Heaven and Earth

The three realms*
Each in its turn
Waxing and waning

Until arriving
At the essence
Of full understanding

Three realms* five times
Who is capable
Of taking such a journey

市人矜巧智
于道若童蒙
倾夺相夸侈
不知身所终
曷见玄真子
观世玉壶中
窅然遗天地
乘化入无穷

Gan Yu - 5

City folk think
They're so damn smart
Treating followers of the Way
As naive and uncouth

Inclined to extravagant boasts
And imposing their will via
Endless harangue

Ignorant of the nature
Of their own human flesh
And mortality's limits

How can they hope to perceive
The Dark Mysteries
Or Truth and its offspring

Or begin to see the world
As it truly is —
An enormous jade pot
In the middle
That's deep and wide enough
To contain Heaven
And Earth

Where we can enter
The realm of the boundless
And make passage through
The entire cycle of changes

吾观龙变化
乃知至阳精
石林何冥密
幽洞无留行
古之得仙道
信与元化并
玄感非象识
谁能测沈冥
世人拘目见
酣酒笑丹经
昆仑有瑶树
安得采其英

Gan Yu – 6

I beheld the Dragon pass
Through the Cycle of Changes
To the point of knowing
The essence of the Yang
And also traveled to
Darkest depths of the
Stone Forest and into
The Cave's deepest recess
Of which no record remains

Such was the knowledge
Of the ancients
Who attained the Way
Through living in the realm
Of cosmic Union and Change
They attained Dark Mysteries
Beyond ordinary comprehension

Today how can we begin to fathom
Such profound darkness
When the common sort are
Constrained by plain sight
Or act as if drunk with delight
In their pursuit of the Immortal Elixir
But on Kun Lun Mountain
There is a Tree of Jasper
To calmly pluck its fruit
It takes a hero

吾观昆仑化
日月沦洞冥
精魄相交会
天壤以罗生
仲尼推太极
老聃贵窈冥
西方金仙子
崇义乃无明
空色皆寂灭
缘业定何成
名教信纷藉
死生俱未停

Gan Yu – 8

I have seen
Kun Lun Mountain
Pass through its Changes
And the Sun and Moon
Fall into the Primal Dark

So the soul's essence
Coheres to find meaning
With all it encounters
On Heaven and Earth

Though Confucius spurned
These Ultimate truths
Old Dan* with
His ears pendant
Relished the Void

From the West
The golden Spirits come
From a sublime height
They descend and
Lose their luster

For in the great Void
All color fades
And becomes
Indistinct

So Karma ordains
Everything comes round
In the end

While great teachers
Proclaim through faith
Disorder too may be
Overcome

But it's always the same
Life and Death
In succession
Without end

玄天幽且默
群议曷嗤嗤
圣人教犹在
世运久陵夷
一绳将何系
忧醉不能持
去去行采芝
勿为尘所欺

Gan Yu – 20

The dark mystery
Of Heaven
So remote
And silent too

The crowd babbles on
Jeering and leering
Ignoring the sages

So the world has gone
For a long time heading
Straight downhill

We need a sturdy rope
To stay tethered
And still we must worry
About getting drunk
And losing grip

On we go
Down the path
Plucking the wild grass
It's not the earth
That deceives us

The Chan Origin Story in Verse

As a spiritual tradition that largely spurned the notion of authoritative scripture, Chan (as well as Zen, Seon and the offshoots and schools that derive therefrom) has instead emphasized personal or direct transmission of spiritual knowledge from master to disciple as the primary means of propagating the faith. To this day, Chan and Zen practitioners emphasize their spiritual descent or lineage through which they can trace the transmission of spiritual authority and insight all the way back to the original Chan patriarch. Bodhidharma is the Indian monk who is revered as the first patriarch and credited with bringing the seed of enlightenment to China in the 5th or 6th century.

While direct transmission lies at the core of the Chan enlightenment experience, poetry has often played an important ancillary role as a means of expressing and evidencing the personal experience. A poem by a Chan master is nothing more than a purely personal expression of faith. But in a tradition that emphasizes direct transmission of spiritual knowledge, poems are a means by which personal spiritual insight can be shared when personal contact is impossible, a mode of direct personal transmission supervening every day constraints of space and time.

The Chan origin story is a strange mixture of legend and poetry, in which poetry figures prominently in the foundational myths of the Chan tradition. Here, for instance, is a poem attributed to Bodhidharma, the first patriarch:

花種一連串
達摩
吾本來玆土
傳法渡迷情
一花開五業
結果自然成

Flower from Seed in Succession

I first came to this land
To transmit Buddha's teaching
Passing through bewilderment
One flower opens to five schools
An outcome of natural succession

There is no way to know whether Bodhidharma actually wrote this poem. It was more likely written long after Bodhidharma's lifetime, when the five Houses of Chan* alluded to in the next to last line of the poem had all come into existence. Even so, it illustrates the central role poetry played in the development and propagation of the faith, giving personal voice to an otherwise remote figure of legend.

Poetry also figures prominently in the legend surrounding Hui-neng, the Sixth Patriarch, who is the revered as the founder of Chan. According to the account provided in the Platform Sutra, when the Fifth Patriarch, Hung-jen, was preparing to select his spiritual heir, he summoned his disciples and told them: "Return to your rooms and look into your prajna intuition. Then each of you write a poem and bring it to me. I will read your verses, and if there is one who is awakened to the cardinal meaning, I will give him the robe and the Dharma* and make him the Sixth patriarch. Hurry! Hurry!"

According to the legend, most of the disciples expected Shen-hsui, the head monk, to receive Hung-jen's blessing. And indeed, after struggling for many hours with this instruction, Shen-hsui composed the following verse, which he inscribed on the temple wall by candlelight:

身是菩提樹
心如明鏡臺
時時勤拂拭
勿使惹塵埃

The body is a Bodhi tree
While mind stands aloft
Like a bright shining mirror
That must be endlessly
Cleaned with diligence
To avoid any blemish or
The least speck of dust

A fine poem indeed, and ordinarily it might have sufficed to secure for Shen-hsui the coveted position of Sixth patriarch. However, the Fifth patriarch felt the poem failed to reflect the attainment of full Bodhi awareness and he urged the head monk to spend a few more days thinking and then to make some revisions.

Shen-hsui, however, proceeded to fall under the spell of writer's block. Meanwhile, a young illiterate monk, who happened to be working in the threshing room, heard Shen-hsui's verse as it was being recited. Quite suddenly, this illiterate monk, who was known as

Hui-neng, understood the flaw in the head monk's verse and composed his own poem in response. With the help of another monk, Hui-neng's poem too was inscribed on the wall alongside.

菩提本無樹
明鏡亦非臺
本來無一物
何處惹塵埃

> Bodhi is derived
> Without a tree
> Shining mirror or
> Platform of any kind
> But comes from the
> Very essence of nothing
> From whence comes
> So much dust

Hui-neng returned to the threshing room, but his poem created a sensation among the disciples. The Fifth patriarch, upon hearing the poem, realized it demonstrated a near-perfect understanding of the cardinal truth and summoned Hui-neng into his presence. After recitation of the Diamond Sutra by the elder patriarch, Hui-neng immediately became enlightened and received the Dharma. The Fifth patriarch then handed Hui-neng his robe and told him: "This robe is the proof and is to be handed down from generation to generation. My Dharma must be transmitted from mind to mind. You must make people awaken to themselves."

As further related by Chan legend, following the transmission of the robe, Hui-neng fled into the night in order to avoid the jealousy of the other disciples. From that point on, while various versions of the

Sixth patriarch's story have been handed down, the historical record is clear — Hui-neng subsequently emerges as the founder of the Southern School of Sudden Enlightenment, goes on to become perhaps the greatest spiritual leader in Chan Buddhism and, as the Chan tradition itself was transmitted across the South China Sea, eventually becomes one of the most revered figures in Zen Buddhism as well.

Poems of the Literati

Zhang Jiu Ling

Zhang Jiu Ling was a senior government official during the golden age of the Tang Dynasty*. He had a long and distinguished career, was highly regarded for his personal integrity and plain-spoken advice, and served as one of Emperor Xuan Zong's senior ministers. As was typical of many high officials, he was also an accomplished poet.

Unlike the other poets collected in this anthology, Zhang did not seem to have a formal spiritual practice as a Buddhist or Daoist; if anything, he was more of a Confucian, having dedicated his energies first and foremost to government service. Yet some of his best-known poems are strikingly spiritual and contemplative in nature, particularly those fashioned in the manner of Gan Yu. As evidenced in Zhang Jiu Ling's poems, the poetry of awakening transcends the boundaries of any one spiritual tradition. Writing poetry had become a form spiritual practice itself.

感遇其二

蘭葉春葳蕤
桂華秋皎潔

欣欣此生意
自爾為佳節

誰知林棲者
聞風坐相悅

草木有本心
何求美人折

Gan Yu – II

The orchid leaf
So lush in spring
And the cassia
With its brilliant
Autumn flowering

The sheer delight
Of the force of life
As each being unfolds
According to scheme

Whoever takes
A forest perch can learn
These simple pleasures
By sitting and listening
To the wind

As grass and trees
In turn show
Their intentions
Revealing what
Beauty is to man
Before disappearing

感遇三

幽人归独卧
滞虑洗孤清
持此谢高鸟
因之传远情
日夕怀空意
人谁感至精
飞沉理自隔
何所慰吾诚

Gan Yu (III)

Into seclusion returning
A man resumes his lonely perch
Deliberate in manner
Bathed in purity and truth

Like a soaring goose
Feeling full of thanks
Because of the great distance
Spread out underneath
Over which the soul shall pass

Day and night
Mindful of
Emptiness
But can anyone
Attain its essence
Soaring or sinking
From self fully
Detached

Where
Am I to find
Such comfort
Please tell me truly

Yuan Jie

Yuan Jie was a contemporary of Zhang Jiu Ling and also served as a government minister, though never rising to the top-ranks of service. In contrast to Zhang, some of Yuan's poetry reflects a strong Daoist influence. This poem, in particular, reads like a personal gloss on the Chuang Tzu or Dao De Jing.

引极三首
思元极

天旷莽兮杳泱茫
气浩浩兮色苍苍
上何有兮人不测
积清寥兮成元极
彼元极兮灵且异
思一见兮藐难致
思不从兮空自伤
　心慆兮意惶懹
　思假翼兮鸾凤
　乘长风兮上弡
　挹元气兮本深实
　餐至和兮永终日

Reaching for the Extremity

Under Heaven
A forgotten place
Overrun with weeds
Desolate and vast

But the energy
Is utterly boundless
Although ashen gray
It's always flourishing

Ascending there
What a person finds
Is truly unexpected

A storehouse of
Clarity and solitude
Upon attaining that
Prime and utmost spot

At this primal extremity
The spirit quickens
And distinguishes itself

Just consider
Its singular appearance
Meager and troubling
And barely defined

Yet also consider
From this Vacuity
No harm to the Self
Will come

Even if the heart
Grows agitated
And fear rings out

Remember that
Falsity surrounds
The target's center
Of the virtuous heart

It's a long journey
Riding the wind and
Soaring above

Clasp your hands and
Retain vital energy
Hold on to the source
In its richness and depth

Feast there until
You attain full harmony
Which will last forever
And all day

Li Bai

Li Bai is one of the most acclaimed of all Tang poets, revered in China as one of its greatest literary figures, he is one of the few classical Chinese poets whose work is somewhat familiar to readers in the western world. Best known as a romantic and nature poet, and infamous for his carousing and composing poems deep in his cups, Li Bai may seem like an odd choice to be included in this collection. But Li Bai also had a deeply spiritual side, rooted in the Daoist tradition, in which contemplation of nature, meditation and poetry all seem to merge. One of the remarkable aspects of Li Bai's work is that some of his finest poems were composed spontaneously, in the moment and off the cuff, as it were, highlighting yet another way in which poetry and meditation could become part of a unified practice of intense present mindedness.

山中问答

问余何意栖碧山
笑而不答心自闲
桃花流水窅然去
别有天地非人间

Q & A in the Middle of the Mountains

Ask why I stay
So many days
In these blue green mountains

A laugh is my only answer
Leisure fills my heart

As a peach blossom
Falls into the river
To be carried far away
On the current

Apart from Heaven and Earth
From the human realm estranged

独坐敬亭山

众鸟高飞尽
孤云独去闲
相看两不厌
只有敬亭山

On Jing Ting Mountain

A flock of birds
Soars high above
A solitary cloud
Idly drifts by

Beholding each other
We two never tire
Jing Ting Mountain and I

庐山谣

我本楚狂人
凤歌笑孔丘
手持绿玉杖
朝别黄鹤楼

五岳寻仙不辞远
一生好入名山游
庐山秀出南斗傍
屏风九叠云锦张
影落明湖青黛光
金阙前开二峰长
银河倒挂三石梁
香炉瀑布遥相望
回崖沓嶂凌苍苍
翠影红霞映朝日
鸟飞不到吴天长
登高壮观天地间
大江茫茫去不还
黄云万里动风色
白波九道流雪山

好为庐山谣
兴因庐山发
闲窥石镜清我心
谢公行处苍苔没
早服还丹无世情
琴心三叠道初成
遥见仙人彩云里
手把芙蓉朝玉京
先期汗漫九垓上
愿接卢敖游太清

A Song of Lu Mountain

I am the madman of Chu
Who sang for Confucius
And laughed at him too
All the while
In both my hands
A precious jade staff
Tightly I clasped

To Yellow Crane Tower
At dawn I departed
Onto the Five Sacred Peaks
Searching for Immortals
Far and wide

For an entire lifetime
Across Ming Shan
I have wandered there
Then across Lu Shan
Where I approached the Big Dipper
Through the nine screens
Traversing through clouds
Like wind through
A brocade cloth

Out of the shadows
And into brightness
I found a crystal clear lake
Its surface shimmering with
Dazzling colorful rays
And the gates of golden watchtower
Opened silently before me
Revealing in the distance
Two more enormous peaks

Down a winding path I strolled
Where there flowed a silvery stream
Under three stone bridges
It passed and then tumbled
Down a sheer precipice
In a misty waterfall
Obscure in thick with a
Blue green haze

While on the skyline
Clouds glowed persimmon
Herald of the morning sun
And birds beat their wings
In endless flight on their way
To the state of Wu

Ascending these heights
What great vistas have I seen
Of Heaven and Earth
As well as places in between
A river that flows apart from
Space and time
Measureless and vast
Filled with whitecaps
Flowing fast
Yellow clouds
Propelled ten thousand miles
By the relentless wind
Towards nine distant
Snowcapped peaks

This is the song
Of Lu Shan
The spirit that
The mountain speaks

At leisure I gaze
At her rocky crags
As into a mirror
More clearly
It's my own heart
I glimpse

Down pathways
Long overgrown
Moss everywhere
A thick dark green
Taking an extra dose
Of cinnabar tablets
Beyond this world
The heart stirs
Like a zither
Strummed three times
It trills from
First to last

And far in the distance
See the Immortals assembling
Filled with roseate inner light
In their hands they hold
Hibiscus blossoms
To present the Jade Emperor
In the Imperial Court

Before crossing the void
Nine levels ascending
At last arriving
At the truth of Lu
Approaching utter clarity
Though the work continues
Onward still

Wang Wei

Wang Wei is also considered one of the Tang periods greatest literary figures, almost as highly regarded as Li Bai; in addition, he was an accomplished painter and musician. As with many other well-known Tang poets, he had a long career in government service, rising and falling out of favor with the Emperor and his senior ministers. In later years, he devoted himself more to his Buddhist spiritual practice and spent a decade in retirement, studying with a Chan master.

Wang Wei is best known for his nature poems and vivid landscapes. As Su Shi (another equally famous Chinese writer) observed, Wang's poems hold a painting within them, just as his paintings contain a poem. There is also a distinctive spiritual quality to the landscapes Wang depicts, as you can see from the selection of poems below.

鹿柴

空山不见人
但闻人语响
返景入深林
复照青苔上

Deer Park

An empty mountainside
No one to be seen
But the echo of voices resounds
Sunlight reaches deep into the woods
Once more the green moss glistens

愚公谷三首

一

愚谷与谁去
唯将黎子同
非须一处住
不那两心空
宁问春将夏
谁论西复东
不知吾与子
若个是愚公

二

吾家愚谷里
此谷本来平
虽则行无迹
还能响应声
不随云色暗
只待日光明
缘底名愚谷
都由愚所成

三

借问愚公谷
与君聊一寻
不寻翻到谷
此谷不离心
行处曾无险
看时岂有深
寄言尘世客
何处欲归临

The Yu Gong Valley

I.

Heading into a valley
Quite simply traveling
With nobody but
Master Li for company

Nothing is needed
For either of us
Except a place to sleep
Empty and carefree

Regardless whether
It's spring or summer
Or which way east or west
Happens to lie

Unknowing
Just like a child
That's how it feels
Lowly and lofty
At the same time

II.

A simple home
In a simple valley
A valley at first that
Looks so unbecoming

Although we travelers
Leave not a trace

Still the valley resounds
With an answering cry

And to a cloudless sky
Comes the onset of darkness
Followed soon enough
By day's bright return

Here's the true meaning
Of this place
Simple valley
From simplicity itself
Everything else derives

III.

To find this valley
So lofty but plain
Depends on nothing
But a careful search

Not looking all over
For some remote spot
Because this place
Lies close at hand

Traveling once
It can be reached
Without much trouble
But to abide in its presence
Requires greater effort

Living by the word
As a mortal guest
When desire takes hold

It's to this simple place
The mind returns

过香积寺

不知香积寺
数里入云峰
古木无人径
深山何处钟
泉声咽危石
日色冷青松
薄暮空潭曲
安禅制毒龙

Passing the Incense Temple

Passing the Incense Temple
On a journey of unknowing
Deep into the cloudy peaks
Alone among ancient trees
A distant bell resounds

Down a steep rocky path
The mountain stream tumbles
Through a dim pine glade
In the fading light of day

Before rounding a bend
It settles in a pool of quiet
Where the peace-filled mind
At last stills the lashing dragon

终南山

太乙近天都
连山到海隅
白云回望合
青霭入看无
分野中峰变
阴晴众壑殊
欲投人处宿
隔水问樵夫

In the Zhongnan Mountains

Taiyi* reaches Heaven
Already it seems and
From there the mountains
Run down to the sea

White clouds encircle
The highest peaks
Merging them together
Sky and cloud intermixed
Obstructing the view

The boundaries among
The peaks grow indistinct
Shadow and light
Crowd together
Filling up the ravines

Hoping to find
Lodging for the night
From across the river bank
I call to an old woodcutter

夏日过青龙寺谒操禅师

龙钟一老翁
徐步谒禅宫
欲问义心义
遥知空病空
山河天眼里世界法身中
莫怪销炎热能生大地风

A Summer Visit to Azure Dragon Monastery to Visit Chan Master Cao

A feeble old man
Walks slowly
Through the Chan temple
Come to pay respects

Yearning to inquire about
The meaning at the heart of meaning
And to reach understanding of
Emptiness that lacks all emptiness

Mountains rivers and sky
All beheld within the eye
The entire world resides
Inside the body of Dharma

There's nothing strange
Everything melts in scorching heat
And soon it will be reborn
From the union of wind and earth

Bai Juyi

Bai Juyi was another celebrated poet of the mid-Tang Dynasty* with a long and distinguished career in government service. Born in 772, he had the advantage of coming of age after the An Lushan rebellion* had subsided, but his career was nonetheless subject to various ups and downs, with periods spent in exile due to factional in-fighting in court.

Bai was one of the more prolific poets of the mid-Tang period, with 2,800 poems in his collected works. His poems address wide-ranging themes, mostly secular in nature. But throughout his life Bai showed consistent interest in both Daoism and Buddhism, and frequently wrote about visiting monasteries and his friendship with various monks. In his later years he became increasingly involved with Chan Buddhism and, after retirement from government service, spent more than a decade living in the Longmen Monastery, where he became known as the Hermit of Xianshang, and his poetry revolved around spiritual themes.

Bai's poetry is in a plain-spoken, highly accessible style, which helped make him one of the most popular writers during his lifetime. The spiritual poems he wrote in his later years are more abstruse and imbued with a sense of the ineffable that lies at the heart of the Chan experience.

白云泉

白居易

天平山上白云泉
云自无心水自闲
何必奔冲山下去
更添波浪向人间

White Cloud Nursery

Up in the plains of Heaven
Above the mountaintops where
White clouds spring to life

To speak of what comes forth
Without the least effort
Flowing naturally as from
The soul at rest

Never rushing
Nor hurtling headlong
Against the mountains
Down below

Being continually replenished
A tidal wave from heaven
That sweeps towards earth

老去

老去愧妻儿
冬来有劝词
暖寒从饮酒
冲冷少吟诗
战胜心还壮
斋勤体校羸
由来世间法
损益合相随

Growing Old

Growing old and departing
Leaving wife and child behind
But when winter arrives
Consolation comes via poetry

Warmth and chill both derive
From the same swig of wine
But the chill is diminished
Reciting a poem's first lines

To surmount the mind
Still calls for struggle
Through diligent fasting
The body retains lean form

From the beginning of time
So the Dharma* ordains
Increase and decrease are
Conjoined and entrained

秋斋

晨起秋斋冷
萧条称病容
清风两窗竹
白露一庭松
阮籍谋身拙
嵇康向事慵
生涯别有处
浩气在心胸

Autumn Fast

At daybreak arising to
Prepare for a cold autumn fast
The desolate scene
Suited to my bleak mood

A cool breeze at both windows
Stirring in the bamboo grove
And white dew coats the pine
In the courtyard below

As Ruan Ji* schemed
To appear inept and drunk
And Ji Kang* pursued
Health through rest

So at this point in life
Following my own path
I conjure a vast spirit residing
In each heartbeat and breath

秋夜独坐

独坐悲双鬓
空堂欲二更
雨中山果落
灯下草虫鸣
白发终难变
黄金不可成
欲知除老病
唯有学无生

Autumn Evening Sitting Alone

Sitting alone in sadness
Both temples furrowed
In an empty room
Awaiting second watch

There's rain in the mountains
Where the fruits have fallen
And beneath the lamplight
Crickets cry in the damp grass

Hair grown white
From root to end
Is just as hard to transform
As the purest gold

Yearning for knowledge
To expunge age and illness
But who can attain the wisdom
Beyond birth and death

谈禅境

须知诸相皆非相
若住无余却有余
言下忘言一时了
梦中说梦两重虚
空花岂得兼求果
阳焰如何更觅鱼
摄动是禅禅是动
不禅不动即如如

Speaking About Chan

What you must know is
Nothing is as it seems
What appears lacking
Overflows in abundance

Forget a word's meaning
And it will be understood
In a dream to speak of dreaming
Emptiness is doubled

How does an empty flower
Yield twice as much fruit
How do you find fish
Amidst a desert mirage

Restrain movement in
Meditation's stillness yet
Meditation is movement still
Not meditating
Not moving
Such as it is

道场独坐

整顿衣巾拂净床
一瓶秋水一炉香
不论烦恼先须去
直到菩提亦拟忘
朝谒久停收剑佩
宴游渐罢废壶觞
世间无用残年处
只合逍遥坐道场

Sitting Alone in Meditation

Clothes neatly folded
Dust brushed from the bed
A pitcher of clear water
Incense fills my head

All former worries
Shall be released
To arrive at Bodhi
All plans forgotten

Customs of court long ago ceased
Laying aside sword and sheath
No more wandering
Farewell to the feast

Worldly things of no avail
Time and place in disrepair
Only sitting just sitting brings
Unfettered freedom and peace

Poems by Hermits, Monks and Chan Masters

Han Shan

Han Shan, or the Poet of Cold Mountain, is perhaps the best known of the hermit poets of the Tang Dynasty*, although there remains considerable doubt whether there ever lived any such single poet by that name. Rather, Cold Mountain is part of the Tian Tai mountain range in Chekiang Province where a number of Daoist and Chan hermits sought refuge throughout the Tang Dynasty. According to legend, a monk named Han Shan and his simpleton companion named Shide were together the authors of about 600 poems, half of which have survived to the present day. But there is no historical record of any such persons and it is equally plausible that the poems were the work of various hermits and monks who lived in the Cold Mountain region, a remote mountainside in 9th century China.

可笑寒山道
而无车马踪

联豀难记曲
叠嶂不知重

泣露千般草
吟风一样松

此时迷径处
形问影何从

It's funny how
Cold Mountain path
Proceeds along
Without a trace of
Horses and carts

As the streams
Run together
It's hard to remember
Each twist and turn
That brought you here
And the layers of peaks
That loom in the distance
Unknowable

The dew weeps
Upon a thousand
Blades of grass
And the wind moans
With the pines as one

At the moment when
The path seems to disappear
Shape turns to ask shadow
From whence it has come

智者君抛我
愚者我抛君
非愚亦非智
从此断相闻

入夜歌明月
侵晨舞白云
焉能拱口手
端坐鬓纷纷

The sages ignore me
I ignore fools as well
Being neither foolish nor wise
But refraining from all
Such mutual name-calling

I sing to the bright moon at nightfall
And dance with the white clouds at daybreak
I strive to hold my hands in an open *mudra**
Sitting upright with all the uncountable
Hairs on my head

吾心似秋月
碧潭清皎洁
无物堪比伦
教我如何说

My heart shines
Like the harvest moon
A deep pool of clear light
Nothing else has such clarity
For teaching me what to say

岩前独静坐
圆月当天耀
万象影现中
一轮本无照

廓然神自清
含虚洞玄妙
因指见其月
月是心枢要

Meditating in front
Of a rocky cliff under the
Glow of the full moon
It's brilliant as day time
Everything casts a shadow
But without inherent light

The spirit is a vast void
Naturally clear
Emptiness contained
Such as in the depths
Of a mysterious cave
The cause that makes
The moon visible also makes
The moon a pivot on which
The heart's yearning turns

浩浩黄河水
东流长不息
悠悠不见清
人人寿有极

苟欲乘白云
曷由生羽翼
唯当鬒发时
行住须努力

The Yellow River's waters
Boundless and vast
Flow east
Unceasingly
To the ends of time
You'll never see the waters
Settle clearly

But every human life
Has a fixed limit
And the only way to travel
Upon white fleecy clouds
Is to be born with wings
No matter how great
An effort you may otherwise make
Traveling or staying in place
Even though you start
At the earliest age

有身与无身
是我复非我
如此审思量
迁延倚岩坐
足间青草生
顶上红尘堕
已见俗中人
灵床施酒果

Endowed with self or
Once again unbounded
In this way
Thoughts come and go
As for a long while
Under this rock ledge
I sit completely relaxed
My foot extends lifeless
Amidst these shoots
Of soft green grass
Here at the very summit
The mortal world
Falls into decay
And following
The custom
Among mankind
Fresh wines and fruits
Are now bestowed
Upon the deathbed

Shide

According to legend, Shide was the simpleton sidekick of Han Shan who worked in the kitchen of the monastery on Cold Mountain. As you can see from the selection of the poems translated below, for a simpleton, he had a concise and nicely developed poetic style.

诸佛留藏经
只为人难化
不唯贤与愚
个个心构架

The many Buddhas
Left us with scriptures
To help humankind
With the difficulties of
The transformational task
Not just for the virtuous
But also for simpletons like me
So each of us can build
A structure that endures
In our heart

造业大如山
岂解怀忧怕
那肯细寻思
日夜怀奸诈

If you want to build
Something grand
As a mountain
How can you
Be distracted
By worry and fear
You must be able
To focus on a slender thread
Day and night the mind
Works its treachery

昨日设个斋
今朝宰六畜
都缘业使牵
非干情所欲

Yesterday was a day for fasting
Today we slaughter animals to feast
Always led along by custom and practice
Not in accord with actual feeling or need

一度造天堂
百度造地狱
阎罗使来追
合家尽啼哭

For each time we make a paradise
A hundred times we make a hell
Yet if the King of Hell comes after us
The whole household loudly begins to wail

出家要清闲
清闲即为贵
如何尘外人
却入尘埃里

To be a monk calls for some idleness
But such idleness comes at a price
Just as dust gathers on man's outside
So too the dust enters within

一向迷本心
终朝役名利
名利得到身
形容已憔悴

Bewildered always by the heart's core
The end result of serving fortune and fame
No matter what the personal rewards
Soon comes a wan and sallow appearance

Feng Gan

Feng Gan was another monk who according to legend was an associate of Han Shan and Shide. His name literally means big stick and he was supposedly a towering figure often depicted riding on the back of tiger, suggesting a severity of character which comes through in the poem below.

赠诗僧怀静

几生余习在
时复作微吟

坐夏莓苔合
行禅桧柏深

入山成白首
学道是初心

心地不移变
徒云寒暑侵

A Poem for a Monk with an Unyielding Heart

Over several lifetimes
In practice spent
Time and again
Composing the
Profoundest chants

Sitting in summer at one
With berries and moss
Walking in Chan through
Juniper and cypress forests

Entering deep into mountains
Where snow engulfs your head
Studying the Way still remains
Your beginner's intent

Heart and mind firmly grounded
Steadfast and untransformed
A true disciple oblivious to
The incursion of heat or cold

Master Yongjia Xuanjue

Yongjia Xuanjie was a Chan master of the 7th century, a disciple of Hui-neng, the Sixth Patriarch. This enlightenment poem is reminiscent of Hui-neng's earlier poem.

永嘉禪宗
稽首圓滿遍知覺
寂靜平等本真源
相好嚴特非有無
慧明普照微塵剎

Head bowed in perfect repose
Awareness fully dispersed
Tranquil at the center of being
Arriving at the root of peace
Being both easy and severe and
Unique in neither having or lacking
A radiance that illuminates everything
Down to the finest particle of dust

Yongjia is best known for a poem called the Song of Enlightenment, which is less personal in tone and more a recital of major concepts in Chan doctrine and practice. Here is a translation of the first few stanzas of a much longer work.

永嘉大师证道歌

绝学无为闲道人
不除妄想不求真
无明实性即佛性
幻化空身即法身
法身觉了无一物
本源自性天真佛
五蕴浮云空去来
三毒水炮虚出没

证实相 无人法
刹那灭却阿鼻业
若将妄语诳众生
自招拔舌尘沙劫
顿觉了如来禅
六度万行体中圆
梦里明明有六趣
觉后空空无大千

Song of Enlightenment

Abandoning study
Foregoing action
Remaining idle
And following the Dao
Neither avoiding delusion
Nor seeking out truth

Ignorance is
Our real state of nature
In the Buddhist faith
Our temporal bodies once emptied
Become a sacred place

In our sacred body we
Awaken utterly dispossessed
Returning to the origin
In a simple state of grace

The five realms of experience
Are empty and fleeting
Like clouds drifting by
And so too our passions
Which dissipate like steam
Over a boiling cauldron

Looking at things as they really are
Not merely as fancied under human law
In an instant everything can be extinguished
Or consigned to hell on earth

If this sounds like nonsense
Or a deceit upon all living things
Then yank out my tongue
And pile it high with gravel and dust
For an eternity

For just as suddenly when
We awaken to Suchness
In a meditative state we attain completely
The Six Perfections and
Ten thousand good deeds

It's as if we are dreaming
That's how clearly we come to see
The Six Paths of Reincarnation
And only after Awakening thus
Do we confront true Emptiness
Devoid of all Ten Thousand things*

Chan Master Hsiang-yen

The story of Hsiang-yen's enlightenment is a well-known part of the Chan tradition. As recorded in the Wu Men Guan (or Gateless Gate) commentary, Hsiang -yen had been an accomplished scholar of Buddhist sutras, but for many years had made little headway in his meditation practice. One day, his master asked him what his original face had been before birth, to which he could not respond. This question became his personal kōan, and he subsequently burned his sutras due to his inability to resolve the matter. With a begging bowl he set out wandering, until one day, while working in the fields, he heard the sound of a tile striking the ground and attained enlightenment. Similar to the legend surrounding the Sixth patriarch, the following poem is attributed to Hsiang-yen as the record of his enlightenment.

一擊忘所知
更不假修治
動容揚古路
不墮悄然機
處處無蹤跡
声色忘威儀
諸方達道者
咸言上上機

At one stroke
Knowledge is forgotten

The need for dogma and struggle
Forever falls away

The inner spirit is lifted
To the ancient path

Far above the grip
Of worldly despair

The trackless expanse
Extends everywhere

Sights and sounds dissipate
In the presence of simple majesty

Those who reach this
Way in truth

All say it stands above
Everything else

Jiaoran

Perhaps more than anyone else whose work is collected in this anthology, Jiaoran stands right at the intersection of Tang poetry and Chan Buddhism. He was poet and monk in equal measure - an ordained Buddhist monk who was highly acclaimed for the literary quality of his poetry, with more than 400 poems among his collected works. He beautifully expresses the paradox at the heart of poetry that revolves around nothingness.

出游

少时不见山
便觉无奇趣
狂发从乱歌

情来任闲步
此心谁共证
笑看风吹树

Wandering Forth

Time has been lacking
To look upon the mountains
Giving rise to my yearning
For want of their charm
A mad urge to go forth
Amidst my disordered song

This feeling comes round
To resume an idle pace
To nurture thoughts
Quite commonplace
To laugh and watch
The wind as it plays
Upon the trees

投知己

若为令忆洞庭春
上有闲云可隐身
无限白云山要买
不知山价出何人

Seeking Self-Knowledge

As if you could summon forth
Some memory from the cave
Or courtyard of youth

You climb up to find yourself
In idleness surrounded
Your body shrouded in mist

White clouds without limit
Encircle the mountain
No matter how hard you try
To buy it outright

Not knowing the mountain's price
Nor if it will ever come forth
For any man

禅诗

万法出无门
纷纷使智昏
徒称谁氏子
独立天地元
实际且何有
物先安可存
须知不动念
照出万重源

In the Chan Temple

Of the ten thousand Dharmas
Found out beyond the gates
So profuse and confused
Making knowledge seem muddled

Believers look for balance
From one lineage or another
Or else alone pursue truth
Under Heaven and Earth

But in everyday practice
What you possess is prior
To all such things and
In peace abides

True wisdom is found
In the study of stillness and
The light that shines forth
From the origin of
All ten thousand things*

吊灵均词

昧天道兮有无
听汨渚兮踌躇
期灵均兮若存
问神理兮何如
愿君精兮为月
出孤影兮示予
天独何兮有君
君在万兮不群
既冰心兮皎洁
上问天兮胡不闻
天不闻
神莫睹
若云冥冥兮雷霆怒
萧条杳眇兮馀草莽
古山春兮为谁
今猿哀兮何思
风激烈兮楚竹死
国殇人悲兮雨飔飔
雨飔飔兮望君时
光茫荡漾兮化为水
万古忠贞兮徒尔为

Song of the Spirit that Hangs in the Balance

The ways of Heaven remain unseen
Within yet exceeding our grasp
We hear of an island in the stream
But hesitate before entering
In one phase the spirit is balanced
As if it might endure intact
We seek to know more about
The divine that resides within
We yearn to be ruled by spirit
Much as we are ruled by the moon
An image that emerges stark and lonely
Revealing to us what we are

Yet Heaven stays remote
How can we possess its power
Ruling over all ten thousand things*
Yet separate from the flock

So ice grips the heart
While shining in all its glory
Rising up to ask of Heaven
Why won't it pay heed

Perhaps Heaven doesn't hear
Or there are no gods
Just dark clouds obscuring
The sound of the angry thunder
Bleak and desolate
Barely discernible
What remains is no more
Than wild unshorn grass

Who is it that first brought
The ancient mountains to life
Yet today the apes are at a loss
Over what to think
A fierce wind has lashed
The bamboo to death
The country mourns all
The victims of war amid
The chill rains of autumn

Ah the chill rains of autumn
The time of the full moon
Has come round at last
So bright and vast
The moonlight ripples
And transforms
Just like water

So many in number
So old and reliable
The disciples are thus
Left to serve and wonder

寓言

吾道本无我
未曾嫌世人
如今到城市
弥觉此心真

Words in the Heart Residing

My path originates
In what is not me
Never thinking ill
Of humankind
Today going forth
Into the city
Wide awake to
The heart of truth

Five Random Verses

乐禅心似荡
吾道不相妨
独悟歌还笑
谁言老更狂

In the joy of Chan
The heart is swept away
My path seems unhindered
Alone I contemplate and sing
And laugh as well
Who speaks these words
So old and familiar
Yet a little crazy too

偶然寂无喧
吾了心性源
可嫌虫食木
不笑鸟能言

Sometimes by chance
Sitting in solitude
Without the least clamor
I understand clearly
To the very root of
My innermost being
Or else feel as lowly
As an insect feeding on wood
Or not at all smiling
Just chattering
Like a bird

隐心不隐迹
却欲住人寰
欠树移春树
无山看画山
居喧我未错
真意在其间

The mind's intentions
May be completely hidden
But not so its tracks
Which are revealed
Even so how I long
To dwell among the living
At times wooden and
Lacking as a tree
Yet also brought to life
As in springtime
Not to be a mountain
But to look and see
The mountain's image
Residing amidst clamor
Yet not the least mistaken
Between all these intervals
Somehow holding true

虏语嫌不学
胡音从不翻
说禅颠倒是
乐杀金王孙

A prisoner of language
Yet full of regret
If I fail to study
These outrageous sounds
Defying all translation
To speak of Chan
Truly is folly
Joyful yet destructive
To the offspring
Of the Golden King

真隐须无矫
忘名要似愚
只将两条事
空却汉潜夫

To be truly hidden
You must avoid contention
Disregard fame and
Strive to appear dumb
Only by mastering
Both sides of what exists
To be empty yet also
Remain true to
The man within

杂兴

人生分已定
富贵岂妄来
不见海底泥
飞上成尘埃

Miscellaneous Thoughts

Our human life
With its distinct parts
Already determined

Riches and honors
How absurd they are
If ever they come around

Never to see the mud
Of the ocean floor

Soaring on wing
Yet eventually
We're only dust airborne

听素法师讲《法华经》

法子出西秦
名齐漆道人
才敷药草义
便见雪山春
护讲龙来远
闻经鹤下频
应机如一雨
谁不涤心尘

Hearing Plain Truth Spoken In The Lotus Sutra

When the Dharma* came forth
From kingdoms to the west
Its words taken together
Showed us wisdom's path
Conferring healing powers
Through righteousness and virtue
Plain enough for all to see
Like snow on a mountaintop
Or the blossoms of spring
Protecting us when it's spoken
Like a dragon come from a distance
Or an immortal white crane
That descends to help us frequently
When we hear the words repeated
It answers every opportunity
It comes to us just like rain
Not one heart among us
Can't be cleansed of dust

前溪作

春歌已寂寂
古水自涓涓

徒误时人辈
伤心作逝川

Written In Front of a Brook

The happy spring song
Is already gone
The old rushing waters
Are now reduced to a trickle

So too the disciples will
All prove to have been wrong
Soon coming to grief
As the waters recede
For every generation

送灵澈

我欲长生梦
无心解伤别
千里万里心
只似眼前月

To Carry the Spirit Clearly

My yearning for
Longevity is but a dream
Being unwilling to let go
Of human suffering
A thousand miles
Or ten thousand of longing
But all that appears
Before my eyes is the moon

次日

野外有一人
独立无四邻
彼见是我身
我见是彼身

Tomorrow

Out in the country
A man lives alone
Without any neighbors
For miles around
The only thing seen
Is his very own body
And all I can see
Is that body of his

咏皎上人座右画松

写得长松意
千寻数尺中
翠阴疑背日
寒色欲生风
真树孤标在
高人立操同
一枝遥可折
吾欲问生公

A Song Looking Down Upon
A Man Sitting and Drawing
A Picture of a Pine Tree

With a brush hoping to fix forever
The idea of a pine tree
Trying innumerable times
To hit just the right note
Yet what lurks in the blue green shade
Never emerges into full daylight
A shiver of desire born of the breeze
The real tree remains untouched
The mark of existence itself
Yet with enough practice a person
Of talent can grasp the same thing
As if a single remote branch
Could be snapped off
And then how I yearn for it
To be transplanted and given
A new far more public life

送僧之京师

绵绵渺渺楚云繁
万里西归望国门

禅子初心易凄断
秋风莫上少陵原

Poem for Master Jing

To the horizon without interruption
The clouds are arrayed vast in number
Thousands of miles to the western border
Extending to the gates of the empire

In meditation how discrete the task
A beginner's mind focused on withdrawal
Yet the harvest of practice is unsurpassed
In retrieving what is buried within the origin

哀教

本师不得已
强为我著书

知尽百虑遣
名存万象拘

如何工言子
终日论虚无

伊人独冥冥
时人以为愚

The Lament of Learning

The roots of instruction
Are not ours to choose
That which compels me
To write these poems

To be aware to the utmost
Always thinking and pursuing
The right name to capture
Every aspect of existence

But skill with words
Is really not so much
All day long discussing
Nothing but nothingness

One person alone
Immersed in darkness
The time a man spends thinking
May just make him stupid

闻钟

古寺寒山上
远钟扬好风
声馀月树动
响尽霜天空
永夜一禅子
泠然心境中

Hearing the Bell

An old temple stands
On a cold mountaintop

A distant bell carries
Distinctly on the wind

The sound lingers as the moon
Rises through the tree line

And echoes still as frost
Settles from the empty sky

Its nighttime forever meditating
In the stillness of first watch

Flowing deep into
The center of heart and mind

咏小瀑布

瀑布小更奇
潺湲二三尺
细脉穿乱沙
丛声咽危石

初因智者赏
果会幽人迹
不向定中闻
那知我心寂

A Small Waterfall

A small waterfall
So changeable and strange
A trickle then a torrent
Within just a few feet
First a thin stream
Passes diffusely
In slender veins
Over the sand
Then gathers into
A narrow channel
As it tumbles loudly
Through the rocks

From first cause
A wise man's journey
Follows a similar course
The outcome no less remote
From the progress of his tracks
Not tending towards
The certainty of what's
Obvious or well known
But ending in knowledge
Of what resides silently
In the heart's core

Layman Pang

In the annals of Chan Buddhism there is a notable figure named Layman Pang, who is often compared to Vimalakirti* as an exemplar for pursuing a dharma* path outside the monastic orders. Among other things, Layman Pang wrote a few very fine poems, including the following.

日日事無別
惟吾自偶諧
頭頭非取捨
處處沒張乖
朱紫誰爲號
邱山絶塵埃
神通並妙用
運水及搬柴

Every day the same routine
Only with myself in harmony
Not right or wrong but abiding
Nothing revealed or misplaced
Paying no heed to purple or vermillion
Or the distant mountains beyond the dust
Just the miracle and wonder here and now
Of hauling water and firewood

Jia Dao

Jia Dao was another poet of the late Tang period who spent time as an ordained Buddhist monk. His poems are simple and beautiful although he never achieved recognition similar to Jiaoran as a literary stylist.

尋隱者不遇

松下問童子
言師採藥去
只在此山中
雲深不知處

Searching for a Missing Master

Below the pines
I ask a young lad
Where master has gone
Off to pick herbs he explains
Deep in the clouds
In the mountains midst
No one knows where to

题青龙寺镜公房

一夕曾留宿
终南摇落时
孤灯冈舍掩
残磬雪风吹
树老因寒折
泉深出井迟
疏慵岂有事
多失上方期

In the Hall of Mirrors at Azure Dragon Temple

One night long ago
Taking lodging in a temple
Atop the Zhongnan Ridge
As the sun sank low
I sat alone in the lamplight
Pondering the distant peaks
The stone chimes in silence iced
By the driving wind and snow
The old trees trembled with cold
Their branches snapping
The waters frozen solid
Deep inside the well
Freed of all obstruction but
Held in winter's lethargic grip
How to retain this moment
When so much has slipped
Surmounting space
And time

口號

中夜勿自起
汲此百尺泉
林木含白露
星斗在青天

A Simple Utterance

In the middle of the night
Not quite myself I rise
To draw water from
Deep inside the well
The forest trees
Are bathed in white
The stars shimmer
In the clear sky

送田卓入华山

幽深足暮蝉
惊觉石床眠
瀑布五千仞
草堂瀑布边
坛松涓滴露
岳月沉寥天
鹤过君须看
上头应有仙

Sent to Tian Zhuo in Hua Shan Monastery

Deep in seclusion
With the cicadas at dusk
You awaken suddenly rising
From a stone mattress
A waterfall descends
Thousands of feet below
There's a steady drip from
The side of your straw hut
And from the pines overhead
That envelopes you in fine mist
The moon rises behind
The highest peak
Alone in the night sky
Except for a crane
Crossing over
Look my friend
Atop its back
You can see
An immortal

Qi Ji

Qi Ji was a poet-monk who wrote in the late Tang period, as the dynasty was settling into terminal decline. This poem conveys a sense of the broader social meaning of self-cultivation in politically and socially unstable times.

新栽松

野僧教种法
苒苒出蓬蒿

百岁催人老
千年待尔高

静宜兼竹石
幽合近猿猱

他日成阴后
秋风吹海涛

Newly Planted Pines

By a field near where
The monks have taught
Things grow in accordance
With Buddha's law
Luxuriantly sprouting forth
When disheveled then weeded

In a hundred years
A man grows old but
It will take a millennium
For these pines to
Attain their full stature

Peaceful and proper
In a thick stand they grow
Among bamboo and rocks
The wild apes hiding
In the forest nearby

A day will come when they will
Cast thick shade behind
And when the autumn wind blows
They will sway like an ocean wave

The connection between silence and poetry runs deep, a discovery that can be newly made every time one of us slows enough and settles on the mat. What sometimes emerges from quiet contemplation is a meditative poem, as our thoughts gradually lose velocity and trend towards stillness.

Here's a fine example of a meditative poem by the Chan monk Qi Ji which was written in the late 9th century/early 10th century. Instead of calling this a poem (诗) or using one of the many other standard Chinese synonyms for poetic writing, Qi Ji describes this piece with the phrase 书怀 which I have translated as words inscribed in the heart. This strikes me as a very apt way to describe a poem that serves as a bridge leading us to a place where words no longer suffice.

居道林寺书怀

齐己

花落水喧喧
端居信昼昏

谁来看山寺
自要扫松门

是事皆能讳
唯诗未懒言

传闻好时世
亦欲背啼猿

Along the path to the forest temple
Words inscribed in the heart

There's clamor enough
When a blossom
Falls on the water
In this remote place
Residing in faith
Night and day

Whoever comes to
This mountain temple
Can grasp it
If first they take
Broom in hand
To sweep pine needles
From the front gate

These are the matters
Which should remain
Unsaid except for the poem
Still unformed and
Wordless in your head

Rumor and innuendo
And good news
From the world
The countless desires
That burden us
Along with the cries
Of the forest apes

Glossary

All Ten Thousand Things — 万物. All ten thousand things (and variations of the expression) is a phrase that appears repeatedly throughout Daoist and Chan literature of the Tang Dynasty*. It originates in the Dao De Jing as a way of describing *all of creation* and subsequently becomes a shorthand reference employed by many writers.

An Lushan Rebellion — After falling out of favor with Tang Emperor Xuanzong, General An Lushan launched a rebellion in 755 and swiftly captured the eastern capital city of Luoyang, forcing the Emperor to retreat to the south. At first, it appeared the rebellion might succeed, but in 756 An Lushan's forces suffered a setback at the battle of Yongqiu, which allowed the Tang army a chance to regroup. Several years of warfare and social disruption followed, which brought hunger and hardship to much of the Empire. Due to ongoing internal dissension, Emperor Xuanzong was eventually forced to abdicate in favor of his son, who was proclaimed Emperor Suzong. Thanks to military assistance they received from the Uyghurs and Abbasids, the Tang forces were able to regain the upper hand in the fighting, and gradually encircled the rebel forces. In 761, An Lushan was betrayed and killed by his own son, although the rebellion continued for several more years until the Yan Dynasty eventually collapsed in 763. By the end of rebellion, the Empire lay in ruins. By some estimates, over the course of the conflict, more than half the population died, mostly of starvation. Even though the Tang Dynasty* would remain in power for another for another 150 years, it would never regain the economic and cultural heights of its early years.

Bodhisattva — One of the hallmarks of Mahayana Buddhism is the emergence of the Bodhisattva as a personage who stands as the paragon of the spiritual tradition. A Bodhisattva is someone with great compassion who defers enlightenment for him or herself in favor of helping others achieve enlightenment. Avalokiteśvara (a Sanskrit name) is the paradigm of the Bodhisattva in Mahayana Buddhism, a semi-deity who embodies the virtue of human compassion. As Mahayana practice spread north into China, the Bodhisattva ideal became associated with the goddess Guan Yin (观音),whose name may be loosely translated as she who hears the lamentation of the world.

As the concept is more broadly applied, a Bodhisattva would include not just deities such as Avalokiteśvara and Guan Yin but any person endowed with an extraordinary sense of compassion, which might extend to some of the poets included in this collection.

Dharma — A word and concept with a long and varied set of meanings, associated not only with Buddhism, but also with Hinduism, Jainism and Sikhism. As used in Buddhism, dharma may refer to the fundamental nature of reality, as taught by the Buddha, or it may refer more concretely to the specific teachings of Buddha. Originally a Sanskrit word, dharma literally means what is established or firm and thus carries a strong association with the idea of the underlying law, an idea that carries through into the Chinese term for dharma (佛法)which literally translates as Buddhist law.

Five Aggregates — The idea of the five aggregates is central to Buddhist thought going back to the earliest teachings, deriving from the Sanskrit term *Skandha*. The five aggregates refer to the five modes of personal experience — bodily form, sensory experience, sensory perception, mental impressions and conscious awareness. As the concept developed in Buddhist philosophy, everyone's personal experience consists of nothing more than the aggregation of these five modes of experience. Our sense of self is an illusion: we have no essential identity or existence beyond the aggregation of these five modes of experience. This provides the underpinning for the idea of no-self central to Chan and Zen philosophy.

Five Houses of Chan — Although Chan Buddhism for the most part eschewed formal doctrine and placed emphasis instead on meditation practice and personal experience, five distinctive schools of Chan emerged in China over the years of the Tang and subsequent Song Dynasty, each of them with a distinctive lineage associated with a prominent group of Chan masters — the Guiyang, the Yunmen, the Fayan, the Caodong and the Linji. Two of these lineages have survived to the present day — the Linji school which was transplanted to Japan where it flourished as the Rinzai tradition of Zen and the Caodong school which evolved into the Soto tradition of Zen.

Four Noble Truths — The Four Noble Truths lie at the core of Buddhist thought and practice, somewhat the way the Ten Commandments are central to the Old Testament. Restated simply, they are: (i) life consists of suffering, (ii) the cause of suffering is attachment and desire, (iii) there is a way to end suffering and that is by freeing yourself from desire and attachment, and (iv) to end craving and attachment, you must follow the Noble Eightfold Path.

Mahayana Buddhism — Mahayana Buddhism is one of the three major variants of Buddhism recognized to date, along with Theravada and Vajrayana. Originating in northern India in the 2nd Century CE, the Mahayana tradition spread north across the Himalayas and became central to Buddhism as it is practiced today in Northeast Asia, including China, Korea and Japan. The Theravada tradition is prominent in South Asia, whereas Vajrayana is strongly associated with Tibet. As the Mahayana tradition spread across China both before and during the period of the Tang Dynasty*, it became closely associated with Daoism, giving rise to Chan, Zen and Seon, as important variants within the broader Mahayana tradition.

Mudra — A mudra is a gesture or pose, usually involving the hands but sometimes involving the entire body, which serves as an important part of meditation and yogic practice in Buddhism and Hinduism. In Buddhism, various mudras are associated with specific episodes in the life of Buddha, such as the earth witness mudra, in which one hand rests upon the thigh pointing down to the earth, which relates to the moment of Buddha's enlightenment. The Dhyana mudra is the most typical pose in Buddhist meditation practice — with both hand resting, one on top of the other, facing upwards, the hands and thumbs facing upward form a triangle, which is symbolic of the three jewels of Buddhism — the Buddha, the Dharma and the Sangha (or the community of faith).

Old Dan — One of several nicknames for Lao Tzu, generally considered the author of the Dao De Jing, and revered as the founding father of Daoism.

Ruan Ji and Ji Kang — These were two historical figures from the Three Kingdoms period (220 - 280 AD) who achieved legendary status as members of a group of free-spirited poets and musicians known as the Seven Sages of the Bamboo Grove. They were romantic figures, known for prolonged bouts of drunken carousal, defying constraints and conventions of court life, sometimes idealized by the Tang poets as paragons of the spirit of poetry.

Taiyi — This is a phrase which literally translates as Great Oneness, associated with Chinese religious beliefs predating the arrival of Buddhism in China. Chinese culture and early spiritual practice involved a number of cosmic concepts, deities and omnipotent figures (such as the Yellow Emperor and the Jade Emperor) and it is not uncommon to see references to them incorporated into Daoist and Buddhist literature from later periods .

Tang Dynasty — The Tang Dynasty ruled China for almost 300 years from 618 to 907, with two interruptions in the 8th century during periods of rebellion and usurping claims. The first half of the Dynasty is considered a golden age in Chinese history — a period in which the empire enjoyed domestic peace, prosperity and an unparalleled cultural flowering while managing to substantially expand its borders through conquest. The An Lushan Rebellion (755 to 763) [see above] shattered this period and brought about an irreversible decline during the second half of the Tang.

Scholars typically divide Tang poetry into four periods: early, high, middle and late. Early Tang refers to poetry written during the years from the Dynasty's foundation up to about 700 , including poets in this anthology such as Chen Z'iang. The High Tang period generally runs from 700 to 770, encompassing what many consider the zenith of classical Chinese poetry, similar to the Elizabethan period in English literature. The most famous poets of the High Tang period include Li Bai, Du Fu and Wang Wei. The Mid Tang period runs roughly from 770 through 840 and marks the beginning of the decline of the Tang Dynasty* in the aftermath of the An Lushan Rebellion, including poets such as Bai Juyi and Jia Dao, included in this collection. The Late Tang period runs from 840 to the Tang Dynasty's collapse in 907. This marks a period of accelerating social decline but includes a number of distinguished poet-monks, such as Jiaoran, Jia Dao and Qi Ji, whose work is included here.

The Three Realms — Buddhist terminology can be confusing because there is a proliferation of numbered realms, modes of existence, bundles of personal experience, noble truths and so on. The most extreme example of this may be the Tien Tai school of Chinese Buddhism, which was a precursor to Chan, which espoused belief in 10 realms each of which contains 10 worlds, all 100 of which may be understood through the mode of 10 separate suchnesses, as well as three additional realms of existence, which altogether culminates in there being three thousand realms of existence all contained within a single moment. As I said, it all can get a bit confusing.

To make matters moreso, a term like the three realms has different connotations depending on the context in which it's found. In early Indian Buddhist texts, the three worlds or realms refers to three different realms of karma into which a being may be rebirthed — the world of desire, the world of form or the world of formlessness. On the other hand, Chinese Daoist texts use a similar term (三魂) to refer to three realms of existence, corresponding, roughly, to a hellish, earthly and heavenly realms, without any reference to reincarnation. So in Chan literature, which draws from both Buddhist and Daoist sources, a reference to the three realms may implicate both.

Vimalakirti — Another important idea associated with the Mahayana tradition is the emergence of lay practitioners as central to the faith, equal in importance to those who take vows and join a monastic order. Vimalakirti was a contemporary of the Buddha who embodied the ideal of the lay practitioner, whose virtues are recorded in the Vimalakirti Sutra. Layman Pang is the exemplar of the lay practitioner is Chinese tradition, but the broader community of spiritually minded Tang poets, such as Wang Wei and Bai Juyi, may also be seen as further extensions of this notion.

Fomite

More poetry from Fomite...

Anna Blackmer — *Hexagrams*
L. Brown — *Loopholes*
Sue D. Burton — *Little Steel*
Christine Butterworth-McDermott — *Evelyn As*
David Cavanagh— *Cycling in Plato's Cave*
James Connolly — *Picking Up the Bodies*
Greg Delanty — *Loosestrife*
Mason Drukman — *Drawing on Life*
J. C. Ellefson — *Foreign Tales of Exemplum and Woe*
Anna Faktorovich — *Improvisational Arguments*
Barry Goldensohn — *Snake in the Spine, Wolf in the Heart*
Barry Goldensohn — *The Hundred Yard Dash Man*
Barry Goldensohn — *The Listener Aspires to the Condition of Music*
Barry Goldensohn — *Visitors Entrance*
R. L. Green — *When You Remember Deir Yassin*
KJ Hannah Greenberg — *Beast There—Don't That*
Gail Holst-Warhaft — *Lucky Country*
Judith Kerman — *Definitions*
Joseph Lamport — *Enlightenment*
Raymond Luczak — *A Babble of Objects*
Kate Magill — *Roadworthy Creature, Roadworthy Craft*
Tony Magistrale — *Entanglements*
Gary Mesick — *General Discharge*
Giorgio Mobili — *Sunken Boulevards*
Andreas Nolte — *Mascha: The Poems of Mascha Kaléko*
Sherry Olson — *Four-Way Stop*
Brett Ortler — *Lessons of the Dead*
David Polk — *Drinking the River*
Janice Miller Potter — *Meanwell*
Janice Miller Potter — *Thoreau's Umbrella*
Philip Ramp — *Arrivals and Departures*
Philip Ramp — *The Melancholy of a Life as the Joy of Living It Slowly Chills*
Joseph D. Reich — *A Case Study of Werewolves*
Joseph D. Reich — *Connecting the Dots to Shangrila*
Joseph D. Reich — *The Derivation of Cowboys and Indians*
Joseph D. Reich — *The Hole That Runs Through Utopia*
Joseph D. Reich — *The Housing Market*
Kenneth Rosen and Richard Wilson — *Gomorrah*
Fred Rosenblum — *Playing Chicken with an Iron Horse*
Fred Rosenblum — *Tramping Solo*
Fred Rosenblum — *Vietnumb*
David Schein — *My Murder and Other Local News*
Harold Schweizer — *Miriam's Book*

Fomite

Scott T. Starbuck — *Carbonfish Blues*
Scott T. Starbuck — *Hawk on Wire*
Scott T. Starbuck — *Industrial Oz*
Seth Steinzor — *Among the Lost*
Seth Steinzor — *Once Was Lost*
Seth Steinzor — *To Join the Lost*
Susan Thomas — *In the Sadness Museum*
Susan Thomas — *Silent Acts of Public Indiscretion*
Susan Thomas — *The Empty Notebook Interrogates Itself*
Sharon Webster — *Everyone Lives Here*
Tony Whedon — *The Très Riches Heures*
Tony Whedon — *The Falkland Quartet*
Claire Zoghb — *Dispatches from Everest*

Dual Language
vito m. bonito/Alison Grimaldi Donahue — *Soffiati Via/Blown Away*
Antonello Borra/Blossom Kirschenbaum — *Alfabestiario*
Antonello Borra/Blossom Kirschenbaum — *AlphaBetaBestiario*
Antonello Borra/Anis Memon — *Fabbrica delle idee/The Factory of Ideas*
Tina Escaja/Mark Eisner — *Caída Libre/Free Fall*
Luigi Fontanella/Giorgio Mobili — *L'adolescenza e la notte/Adolescence and Night*
Aristea Papalexandrou/Philip Ramp — *Μας προσπερνά/It's Overtaking Us*
Katerina Anghelaki-Rooke//Philip Ramp — *Losing Appetite for Existence*
Jeannette Clariond/Lawrence Schimel — *Desert Memory*
Mikis Theodoraksi/Gail Holst-Warhaft — *The House with the Scorpions*
Paolo Valesio/Todd Portnowitz — *La Mezzanotte di Spoleto/Midnight in Spoleto*

Writing a review on social media sites for readers will help the progress of independent publishing. To submit a review, go to the book page on any of the sites and follow the links for reviews. Books from independent presses rely on reader-to-reader communications.

For more information or to order any of our books, visit:
http://www.fomitepress.com/our-books.html

www.ingramcontent.com/pod-product-compliance
Lightning Source LLC
Chambersburg PA
CBHW021445070526
44577CB00002B/267